Mommy, Was Your Tummy Big?
By Carolina Nadel

Mookind Press

Published by Mookind Press
1600 South Eads Street, Suite 1034N
Arlington, VA 22202

Watercolor paints and black pen were used for the art.

Library of Congress Control Number: 2007902460
International Standard Book Number (ISBN): 978-0-9792761-0-1

Printed in the United States of America

For Daniel

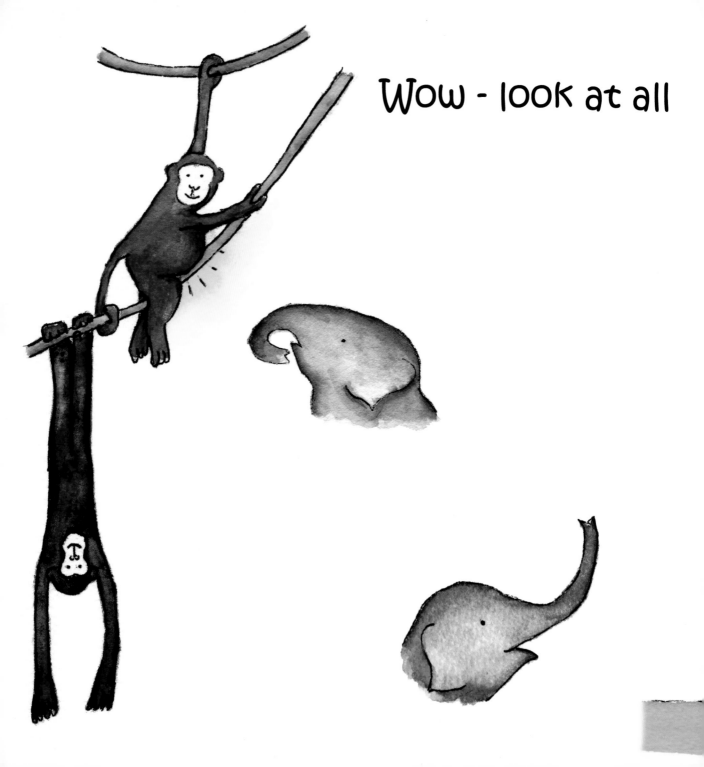

Wow - look at all

the big tummies!

Mommy, was your tummy
big when I was in it?

How did I
get there?

Oh, yes, very big.

Mommy and Daddy wanted to have
a baby like you...

very much.

and no baby came.

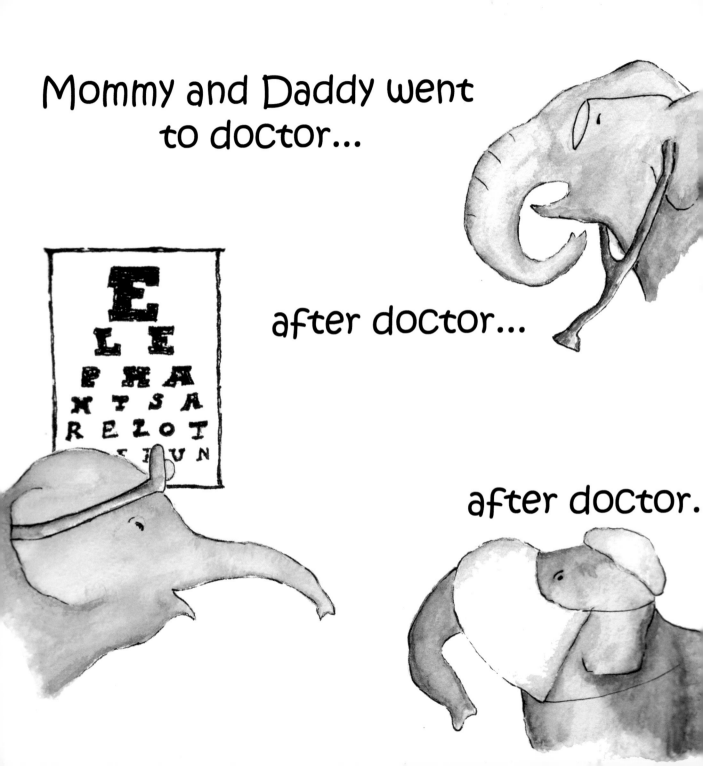

Mommy and Daddy went to doctor...

after doctor...

after doctor.

Had test...

after test...

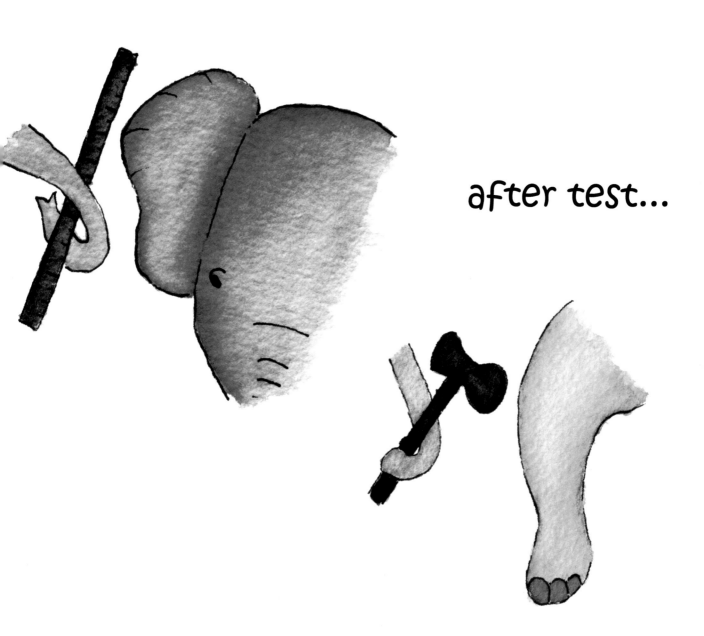

after test.

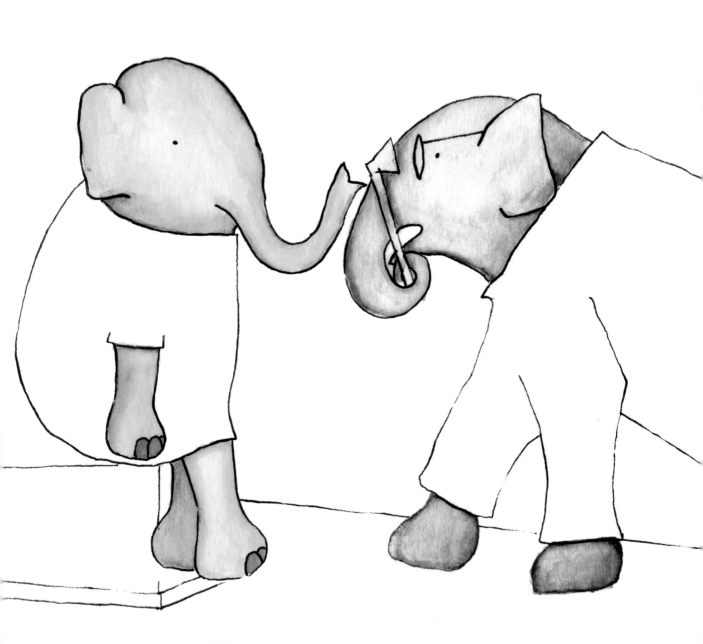

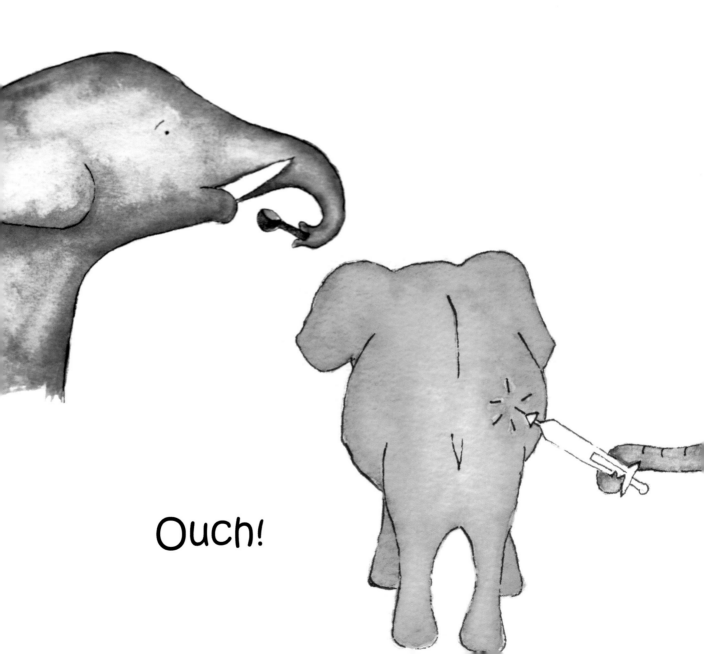

We waited a long time,

We were so

but no baby came.

disappointed.

But, then, doctors helped us find a special lady (a donor) who gave us a small, but very important gift...

an egg.

A doctor put Daddy's cells together with the donor's egg...

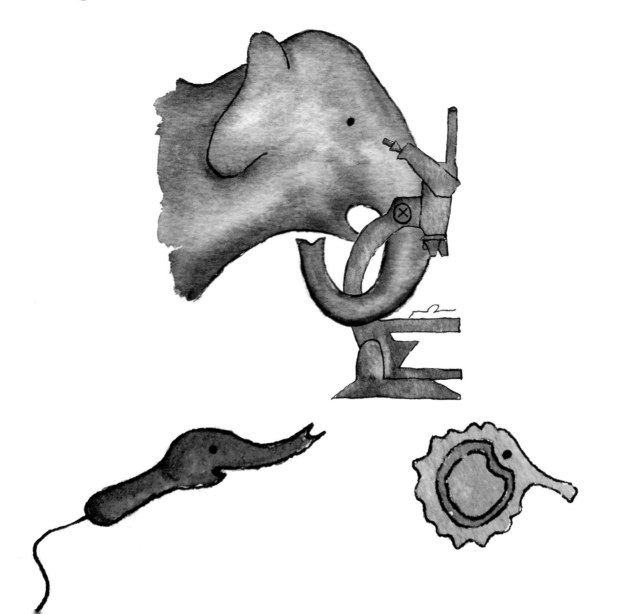

into Mommy's body and
a baby started to grow...and grow...

and grow!

And that was you!   And then
you got big?

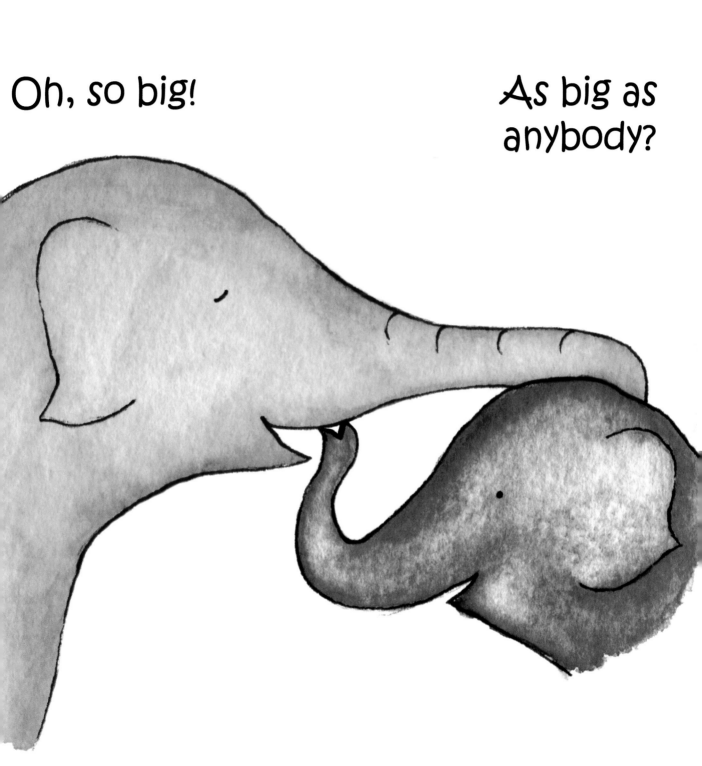

Even bigger than anybody else...

but not as big as my smile!

Carolina Nadel has a background in medicine. She lives in the Washington DC area with her husband and son.

This is Carolina's first book.
Visit her website:
www.CarolinaNadel.com